BEI GRIN MACHT SICH IHR
WISSEN BEZAHLT

- Wir veröffentlichen Ihre Hausarbeit,
  Bachelor- und Masterarbeit

- Ihr eigenes eBook und Buch -
  weltweit in allen wichtigen Shops

- Verdienen Sie an jedem Verkauf

Jetzt bei www.GRIN.com hochladen
und kostenlos publizieren

Bibliografische Information der Deutschen Nationalbibliothek:

Die Deutsche Bibliothek verzeichnet diese Publikation in der Deutschen National-
bibliografie; detaillierte bibliografische Daten sind im Internet über http://dnb.d-
nb.de/ abrufbar.

Impressum:

Copyright © 2009 GRIN Verlag, Open Publishing GmbH
Druck und Bindung: Books on Demand GmbH, Norderstedt Germany
ISBN: 9783668121485

Dieses Buch bei GRIN:

http://www.grin.com/de/e-book/145087/managing-projects-with-feasibility-studies

Arkadi Borowski

Managing Projects with Feasibility Studies

GRIN Verlag

GRIN - Your knowledge has value

Der GRIN Verlag publiziert seit 1998 wissenschaftliche Arbeiten von Studenten, Hochschullehrern und anderen Akademikern als eBook und gedrucktes Buch. Die Verlagswebsite www.grin.com ist die ideale Plattform zur Veröffentlichung von Hausarbeiten, Abschlussarbeiten, wissenschaftlichen Aufsätzen, Dissertationen und Fachbüchern.

Besuchen Sie uns im Internet:

http://www.grin.com/

http://www.facebook.com/grincom

http://www.twitter.com/grin_com

University of Sunderland

BA (HONS) BUSINESS MANAGEMENT

Managing Projects

(SIM 335)

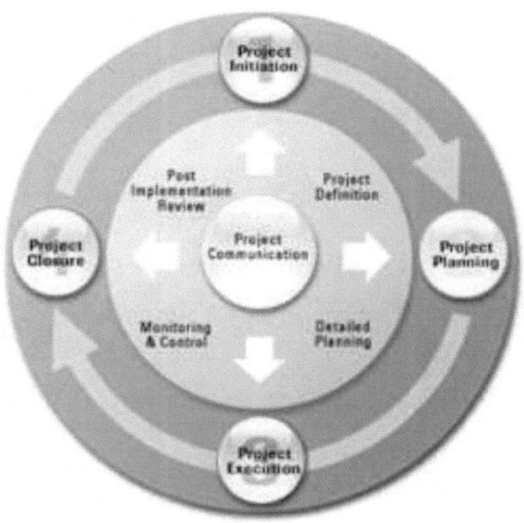

Return date: Friday 9th October 2009

Arkadi Borowski

TABLE OF CONTENTS

1. Task 1

1.1. Exercise 1:

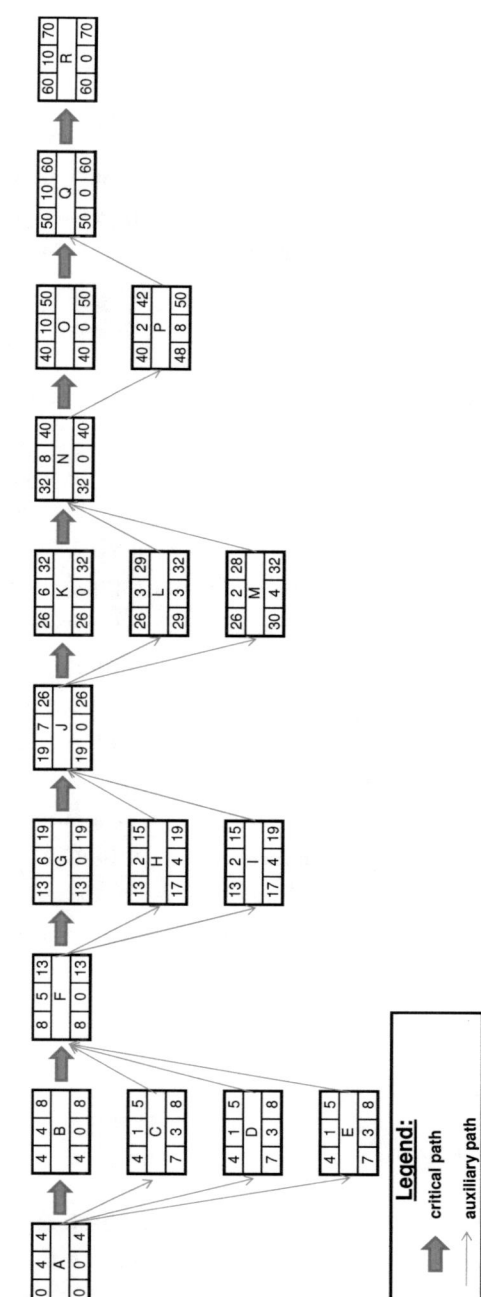

1.2. Exercise 2:

In this project the target is to find out the earliest time, this project could be finished. To calculate the time, I was using the predetermined durations and activities. In the next step of my work I calculated the Finishing – time by using the "forward pass" (*Field M. & Keller L., 2007, pp. 191-198, p. 391*).

> ➢ I used the value zero as the earliest start time for the first activity.
> ➢ If one or more nodes depend on a prior node/one, the node on the critical path is always the node/one with the longest duration.
> ➢ On the critical path the earliest finish time/time to be finished is also equal to the latest finish/- time.
> ➢ There are no total floats on the critical path.
> ➢ You can find total floats only on the auxiliary path.
> ➢ To get the earliest start time, you have to consider the earliest finish time of the prior node.
> ➢ To calculate the earliest finish time you have to add the duration with the earliest start time.
> ➢ To get the total float you have to subtract the total of the duration and the earliest start time from the latest finish time of a node.

1.3. Exercise 3:

The duration of a project is calculated by the critical path which has the influence on the shortest way to finish a project. The latest finish time of the last node on the critical path, is the duration of the whole project. "The critical path activities have no latitude." *(Lewis J.P., 2007, p. 76).*

1.4. Exercise 4:

If the project started on the 05th of April 2010, the project should be ready on the 09th of July 2010. To calculate this you should be aware of the duration of the project. Therefore you have to look on the latest finish time of the last node in the critical path. This project should be ready/ completed after 70 days, so the whole project has to last 14 weeks. Within this project every week includes five working days (a 5 day working week). The expected end of the first week is the 9th April 2010, so I added 13 weeks to that date.

1.5. Exercise 5:

a) The activity "H" is on the auxiliary path and has a total float of 4 days. It has no effect on the duration of the project.
b) If activity "R" is completed one day earlier, the duration of the whole project would decrease by exactly one day, too. The reason for that is that activity "R" is the last one on the critical path.
c) The activity "C" has no effect on the whole project because it is on the auxiliary path and has a total float of 3 days.

1.6. Exercise 6:

A network diagram has a significant importance for this project. It offers the users a better calculation of the time for the whole activities. Furthermore it gives the users many opportunities, for example additional/extra changes of the needed time or additional activities. The importance of the network depends on the duration or quantity of activities. But it is always recommendable to have at least one network because it can spare you a lot of trouble with the deadlines of projects.

By making a network you will have a second chance to prove the feasibility of the project. This means for instance you can avoid, that this project runs out of control, in the sense that the costs or duration of some activities rise above those planned.

Task 1: 592 words

2. Task 2

Before opening a new base

2.1. Executive summary

"Planning begins with an understanding of the assumptions." (*Kerzner H., 2009, p.416*). To start a project it is always important to analyze every step which has to be taken. After studying the steps the next operation includes the control of your resource management, in other words, you have to do a feasibility study. This procedure takes into the account the resources like your team members, the budget and the schedule, which means the time for the project. If you don´t consider or calculate this things, there might occur problems that lead to the result of an unsolvable job.

After it is made sure that the project is feasible, you have/need to minimize the risks, which could endanger the project. This risk for the project could be the budget topping costs or the additional personnel costs for the sick team members.

Furthermore preparing alternative strategies has also to be done. To make this risk management easier you should split your project into parts. Therefore you should use the project life cycle. The Work Breakdown Structure and a network diagram could be also supportive.

The next step consists of the specifying the threats and opportunities. In this phase of your project you need to be aware of the probable problems that prevent you to follow the planned purpose. Additionally it has to be considered about the necessary strategies and help to reach your goals. It is also better to prepare forecasts, to select a strategy portfolio and to prepare action programs. Monitoring and controlling should play a decisive role in your arrangements. (*Kerzner H., 2009, p.416*).

2.2. Introduction

Lax, an SME company, wants to expand. The company wants to move to larger premises creating a new head office there. This change invents a "new one stop shop", where smaller scale organization could call, browse and purchase stationary at their convenience. I am the Project Manager and contracted at the feasibility stage. I am required to prepare a report on how to manage this major project of opening the new base successfully.

2.3. Project Manager

The Project Manager, in this case me, is all along responsible for the whole project, so it is important to have the characteristic trait to lead and to motivate people. "The major responsibility of the project manager is planning." (*Kerzner H., 2009, p.19*). He also has to focus on the project details, to present them clearly internal as well as external.

2.4. Assumptions

As Project-Manager I am reliable for a lot of things, so I need an authorization of wide scope, this means I have to be free to spend money. Also I have to report about the progress of the project to the higher management or rather to the divisional head. To ensure that I have enough members of staff and that they are functional directly responsible to me, I need an authorization to recruit staff. This is necessary because Lax is a small company and consists mainly of sales staff. I need a team of seven members. To be within budget, six members have to be temporary staff. I need them for the decoration of the new store, for the transport and building of equipment and samples. One member of my team has to be my assistant and takes role of the employee of Lax. The assistant will be concerned with PR and marketing work, he also will have to ensure that our customers are invited to the grand opening of the new store and he has to do a daily report to the company head.

My work includes the planning, controlling and monitoring of the project. I have to calculate the budgets for the project activities and to assure the possible risks. The most important work I have to do is, to work out the feasibility study, the project life cycle and the management of finance. Additionally I have to organize meetings with the management of the company weekly to report them the most important facts. Planning the grand-opening of the new store belongs to my function, too.

2.5. Team-Configuration

Organizing and staffing the project-team is always bonded with problems. The project manager needs the right people. This means he needs members with the right qualification on the right place. A big challenge is the size of the team.

"The optimal size is determined by a trade-off between the maximum number of members necessary to assure compliance with requirements and the maximum number for keeping the total administrative costs under control." (*Kerzner H., 2009, p.170*).

Usually the structures of the company handicap the configuration of a team, unless it is a matrix structure. Lax, however is a small company without any structures and has mainly sales staff, so external team members are needed. These members should have different know-hows so that problems could be solved very fast. The project manager should involve every single member in the planning process from the beginning to the end. *(Kerzner H., 2004, p.447)*. Only this way guarantees the most effective work of the team.

2.6. Feasibility study

To start a project without a feasibility study might lead to the unpredictability and so to a lot of unexpected problems. The reason is that the possible dangers for the project had not been taken into the consideration before. Here the question rises up if our company had the opportunities to carry out the project. To answer this you have to make a checklist with details you should know. This checklist should cover themes like: the alternatives, the market potential of the company, cost effectiveness, producibility, technical base and capabilities (state-of-the-art technology), define weaknesses and unknowns and define initial project goals and objectives. *(Kerzner H., 2009, p.419-420)*. If you don´t know what might be the outcome of this study, you should treat it like a separate project with other team members.

Other reasons to do a feasibility study are to convince the head of the company that it is a viable project or to show possible stakeholders like suppliers, customers or the senior management that they can benefit partly from this project.

2.7. Project life cycle

To manage the whole project, to control every single step and to ensure that everything is on time, the project life cycle will be the most important tool for this kind of challenge. "The period between the beginning and the end of a project is usually referred to as the project life cycle." *(Lock D., 2007, p.7).* The project life cycle can be deployed on every kind of project but there are many different ways to reach the planned result. There are life cycles with more than 4 phases, but to keep the project simple and clear, 4 phases project life cycle should be capable in the case of Lax (see figure 1, page 10).

Phase 1: Concept

This stage is the feasibility study. It is needed to define the possible problems and to set targets, to alleviate the following steps. The complexity factor of the next phase is depending on accurate studying of the activities and the results of this phase.

Phase 2: Development

This phase is called "the engineering phase". In this stage you create your team, calculate the finance and review alternatives. The R&D department of the company or a special team dealing with this phase is often included. Here you complete the design of your project on paper, before presenting the project briefly.

Phase 3: Execution

In this stage it is necessary to guide your team through the targets you set up in the last two phases. To minimize risks at their beginning, you have to maintain the plan you worked out.

Phase 4: Transfer

This is the final report stage. The project manager closes all records and prepares the project-relevant data and documents for the handover to the company head.

Figure 1

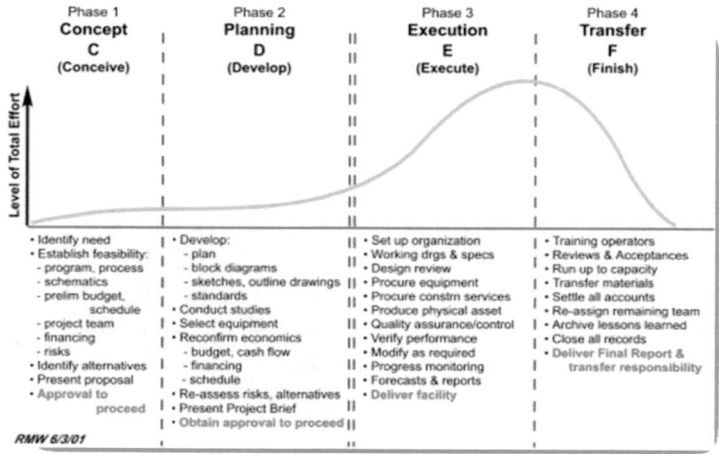

(www.maxwideman.com)

2.8. Finance management

To finish the project successfully it is necessary to control the costs in the specified order. It has to be make sure that the given budget won´t be overrun by not scheduled expenditures. In case of Lax it is important to be correctly within the budget because it is a small company with a small amount of finance resources. This leads to the fact that the project manager has to keep the costs as low as possible. Instigation of

10

financial management implicate a lot of advantages, like risk sharing, achieving economies of scale, lower overall cost of funds, release of free cash flow and even more. *(Finnerty J.D., 2007, p. 25-29).* To get to know if a project is profitable or not, a project manager can use some different techniques.

A very simple but inaccurate method is the payback method. "It shows the time required for the total cash inflows to equal the total cash outflows." *(Lianable O., 2000, p. 113).* It is incorrect on the on hand because it disregards the Return on Investment, but on the other hand it also shows the project manager the extent the project is going to have.

Another technique is the net present value. "Net present value calculates the expected monetary gain or loss on a project by discounting all the projected cash flows to the present using the required rate of return." *(Lianable O., 2000, p. 117).* Here the company can decide if it is profitable to run the project or to put the money in the bank.

The internal rate of return is a popular method to calculate the capital. "Internal rate of return is a discount rate that makes the present value of cash flows equal to the initial investment." *(Groppelli A.A. & Nikbakht E., 2000, p. 159).*

Two more methods with no risks exist there. , the average rate of return and the profitability index and several with risks, for example certainty equivalent factor, risk-free rate and other *(Groppelli A.A. & Nikbakht E., 2000, p. 151-184).*

2.9. Risk management

The fact is there is no project without any risks. So a project manager has to identify possible risks. The sooner a determination of risks happens, the better is the expected result. When all founded predictable risks are identified and registered, is it advisable to think about the decisions which should follow. There are some methods to cover the project against the risk. The company can do it by using contracts with incorporated penalty clauses or defusing the possible risk by using insurances.

2.10. Monitoring & Control

The most important purpose by managing a project is to reach the approved plan on time. So the primary factors are time and money. "During the construction period, advancement of the work is monitored by measuring and reporting field progress at regular intervals." (Clough R.H., Sears G.A. & Sears S.K., 2000, p. 20). This is necessary to stay up to date with the progress. Without controlling the changes and possible risks or opportunities to save money or time a project could grow beyond its original scope. Monitoring and Controlling cover a lot of activities a project manager has to execute. For example: Controlling the information, the progress, the quality, developing work breakdown structures and more. To represent the data and the actual events it is advisable to use charts with cumulative curves, so that everything is clearly arranged. All in all "The road to success is not doing one thing 100 percent better but doing 100 things one percent better." (Brown H.J.Jr., 1988, p. 124).

Task 2: 1908 words

3. List of references

3.1. Literature

Field M. & Keller L, 2007, *Project Management*: The Open University

Lock D., 2007, *Project Management* (ninth edition): Gower Publishing Ltd.

Kerzner H., 2009, *Project Management: A Systems Approach to Planning, Scheduling, and Controlling*: John Wiley & Sons Inc.

Kerzner H., 2004, *Advanced project management: best practices on implementation*: John Wiley & Sons Inc.

Lewis J.P, 2006, *Fundamentals of project management* (third edition): AMACOM

Finnerty J.D., 2007, *Project financing: asset-based financial engineering* (second edition): John Wiley & Sons Inc.

Lianable O., 2000, *The cost management toolbox: a manager's guide to controlling costs and ...:* AMACOM

Groppelli A.A. & Nikbakht E., 2000, *Finance*: Barron´s Educational Series Inc.

Clough R.H., Sears G.A. & Sears S.K., 2000, *Construction project management* (third edition): John Wiley & Sons Inc.

3.2. Internet

Project life cycle (figure 1)

http://www.maxwideman.com/papers/projenviron/dimensions.htm,
Access Date: 3rd October 2009